HAL•LEONARD®
GUITAR
PLAY-ALONG

AUDIO
ACCESS
INCLUDED

ROCK

VOL. 1

T0052750

CONTENTS

PLAYBACK+
Speed • Pitch • Balance • Loop

To access audio visit:
www.halleonard.com/mylibrary

Enter Code
1418-0073-3462-1945

Tracking, mixing, and mastering by Jake Johnson
All guitars by Doug Boduch
Bass by Tom McGirr
Keyboards by Warren Wiegratz
Drums by Scott Schroedl

ISBN 978-0-634-05621-5

Visit Hal Leonard Online at
www.halleonard.com

HAL•LEONARD®
7777 W. BLUEMOUND RD. P.O. BOX 13819
MILWAUKEE, WISCONSIN 53213

Day Tripper

Words and Music by John Lennon and Paul McCartney

D.S. al Coda
(take 1st ending)

Breakdown

Coda

Interlude

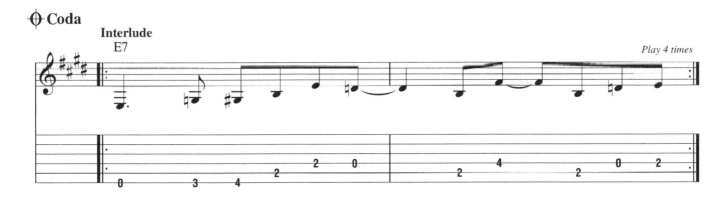

Play 4 times

Outro

Repeat and fade

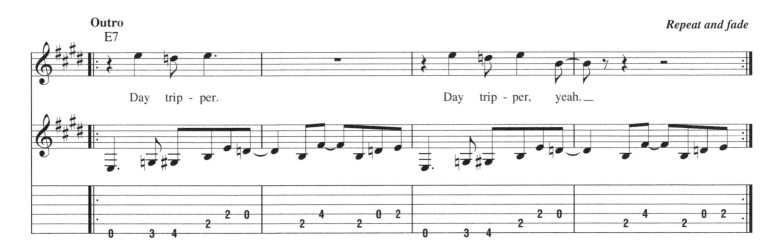

Day trip - per.   Day trip - per, yeah.

Additional Lyrics

2. She's a big teaser.
    She took me half the way there.
    She's a big teaser.
    She took me half the way there, now.

3. Tried to please her,
    She only played one night stands.
    Tried to please her,
    She only played one night stands, now.

Message in a Bottle

Music and Lyrics by Sting

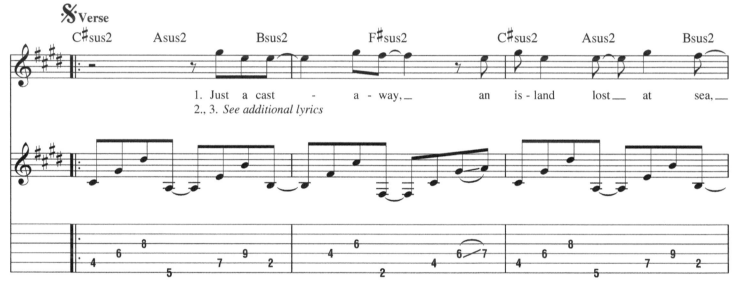

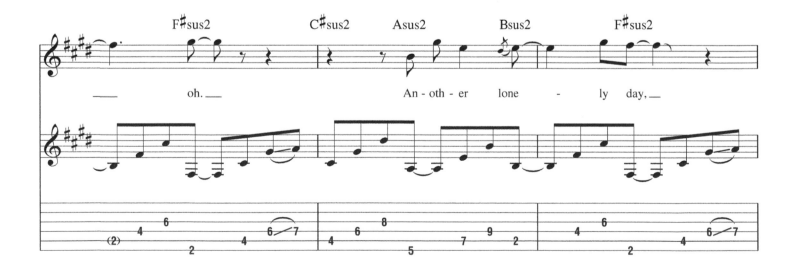

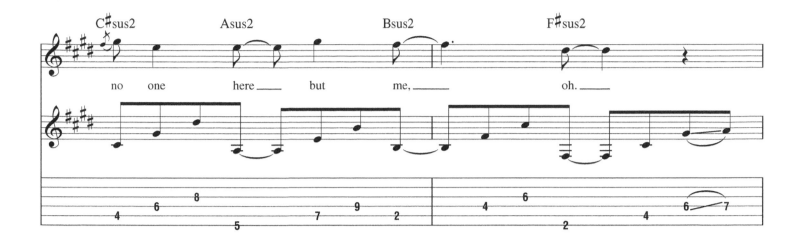

no one   here____   but   me,____   oh.____

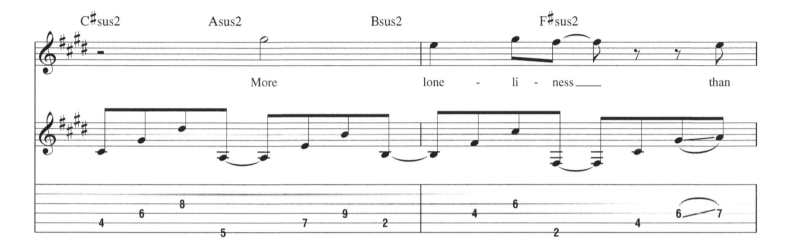

More   lone - li - ness____   than

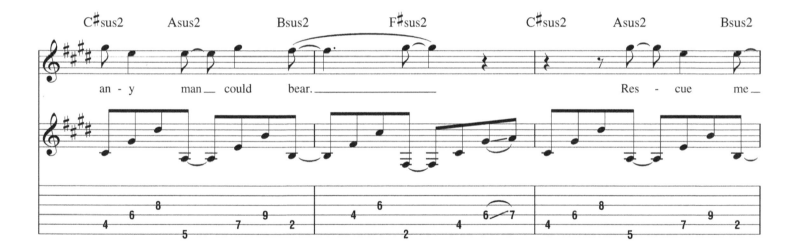

an - y   man____   could   bear._____   Res - cue   me____

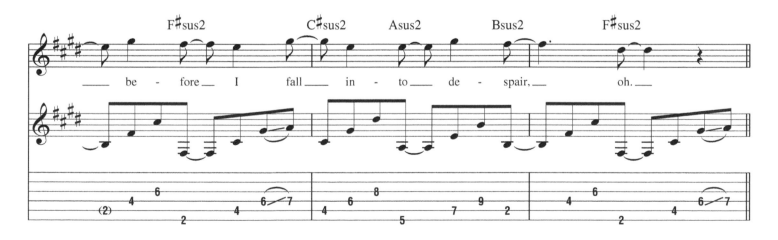

____ be - fore____ I   fall____ in - to   de - spair,____   oh. ____

I'll send— an S.— O. S.— to the world. I'll send— an S.—

— O.— S.— to the world. I hope— that some - one gets— my,

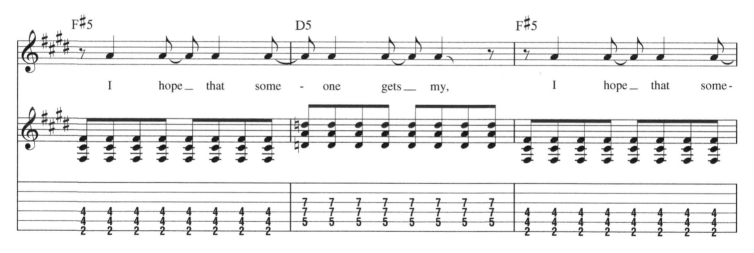

I hope— that some - one gets— my, I hope— that some-

To Coda ⊕ **Chorus**

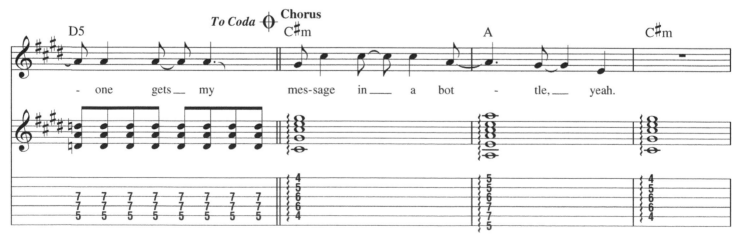

- one gets— my mes-sage in — a bot - tle,— yeah.

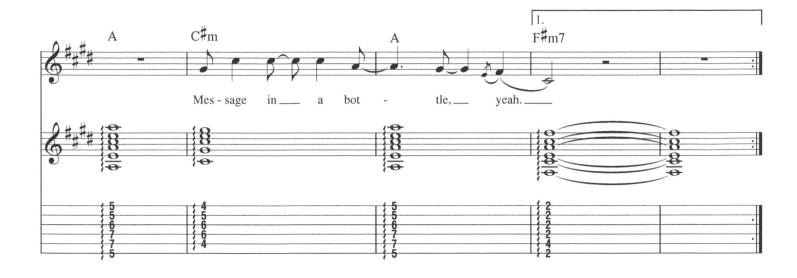

Mes - sage in ___ a bot - tle, ___ yeah. ___

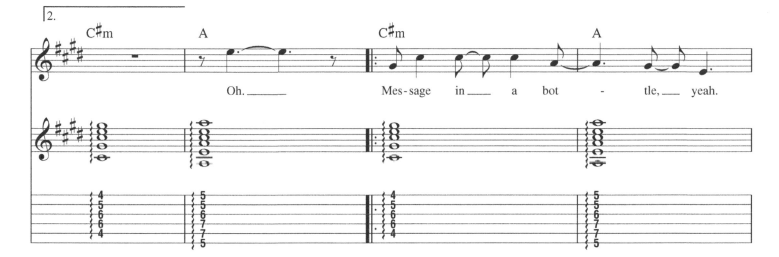

Oh. ___ Mes - sage in ___ a bot - tle, ___ yeah.

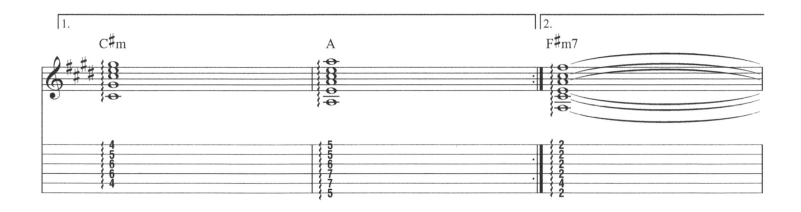

D.S. al Coda

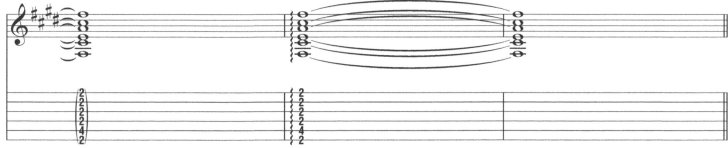

Coda

Chorus

Mes - sage in a bot - tle, yeah.

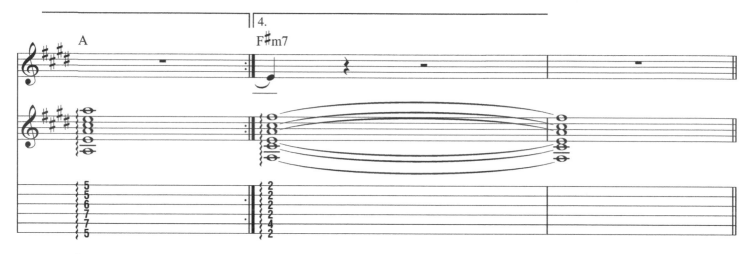

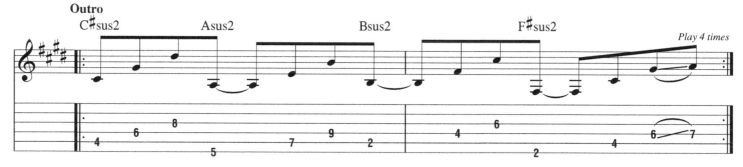

Outro

Play 4 times

Repeat and fade

Send - ing out an S. O. S.

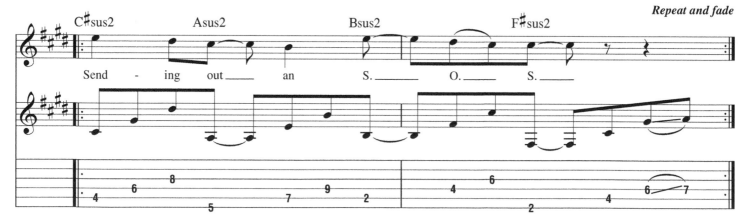

Additional Lyrics

2. A year has passed since I wrote my note.
   I should have known this right from the start.
   Only hope can keep me together.
   Love can mend your life, but love can break your heart.

3. Woke up this morning, I don't believe what I saw,
   Hundred billion bottles washed up on the shore.
   Seems I never noticed being alone.
   Hundred billion castaways, looking for a home.

Shattered

Words and Music by Mick Jagger and Keith Richards

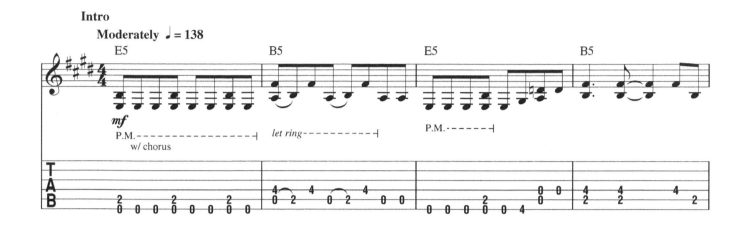

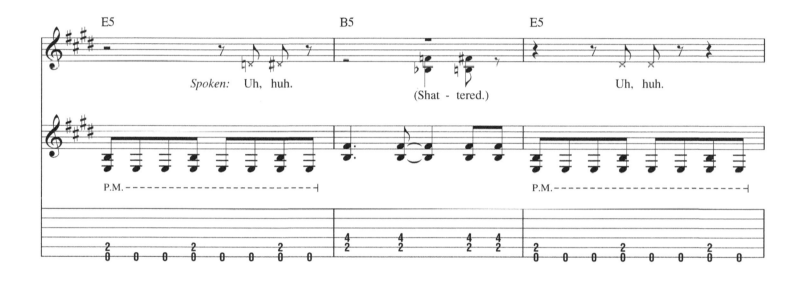

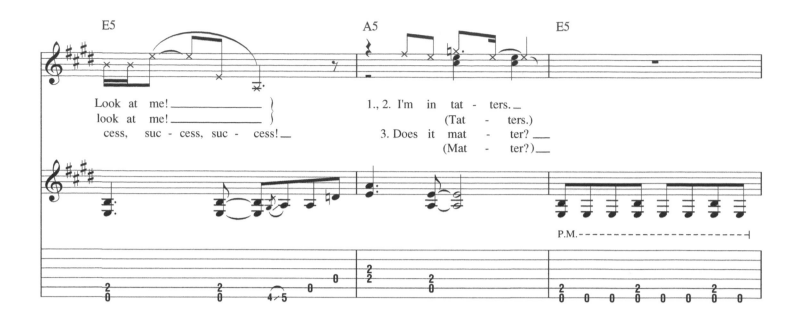

E5 **A5** **E5**

Look at me! ____)
look at me! ____)
cess, suc - cess, suc - cess! __

1., 2. I'm in tat - ters. __
(Tat - ters.)
3. Does it mat - ter? __
(Mat - ter?) __

P.M.-----------------------------------

To Coda ⊕

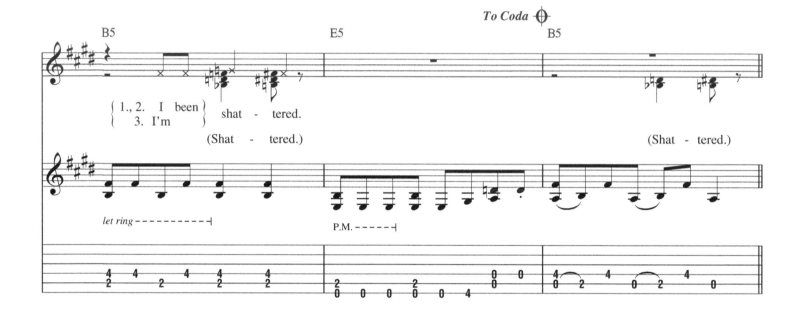

B5 **E5** **B5**

{ 1., 2. I been }
{ 3. I'm } shat - tered.
(Shat - tered.)

(Shat - tered.)

let ring - - - - - - - - - -

P.M. - - - - -

Verse

E5 **B5**

Spoken: 1. Friends are so a - larm - ing and my lov - er's nev - er charm - ing.
Spoken: 2. All this chit - ter chat - ter, chit - ter chat - ter, chit - ter chat - ter, 'bout

P.M.---

let ring---

Life's just a cock-tail par-ty on the street. Big Ap - ple
Shmat - ter shmat - ter, shmat - ter. I can't___ give it a-way on Sev - enth Av - e - nue.___

peo - ple dressed in plas - tic bags di - rect - ting traf - fic.
(Sha - doo - be.)   (Shat - tered.)
___ This town's___ been wear - in' tat - ters.   Uh, huh.
(Sha - doo - be.)   (Shat - tered.)

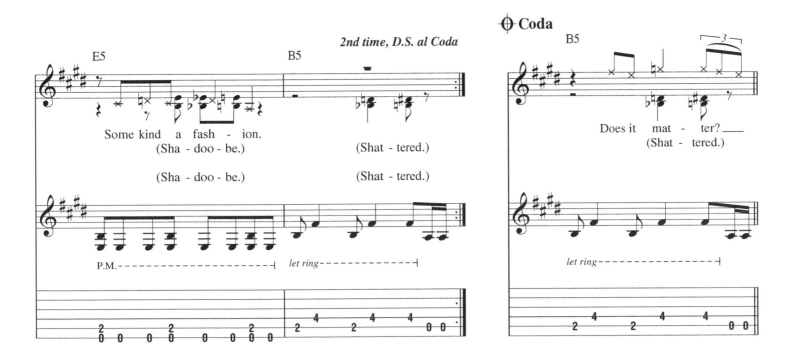

2nd time, D.S. al Coda

⊕ **Coda**

Some kind a fash - ion.
(Sha - doo - be.)   (Shat - tered.)

(Sha - doo - be.)   (Shat - tered.)

Does it mat - ter?___
(Shat - tered.)

Guitar Solo

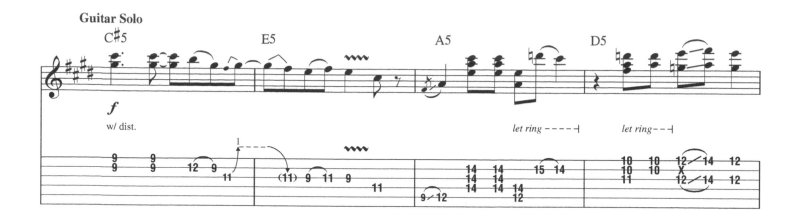

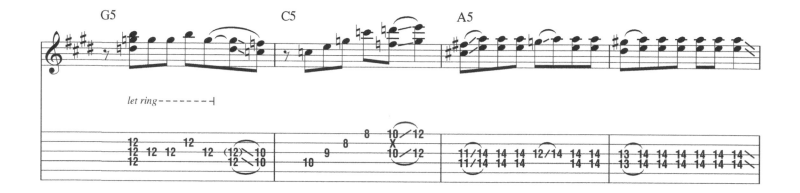

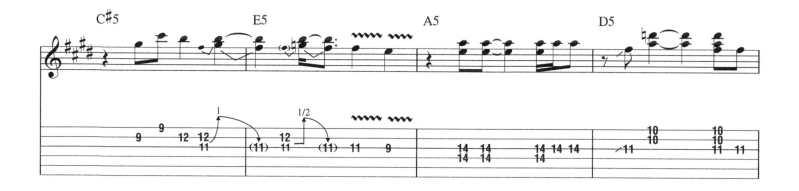

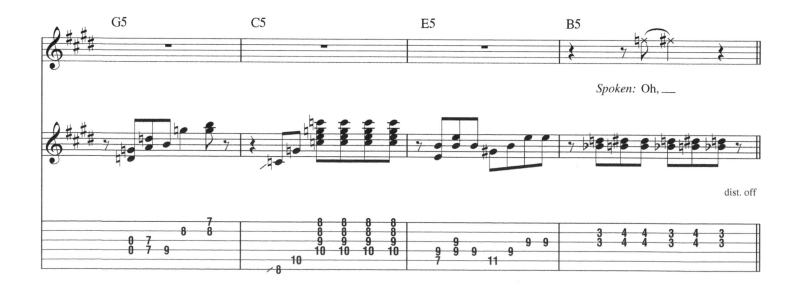

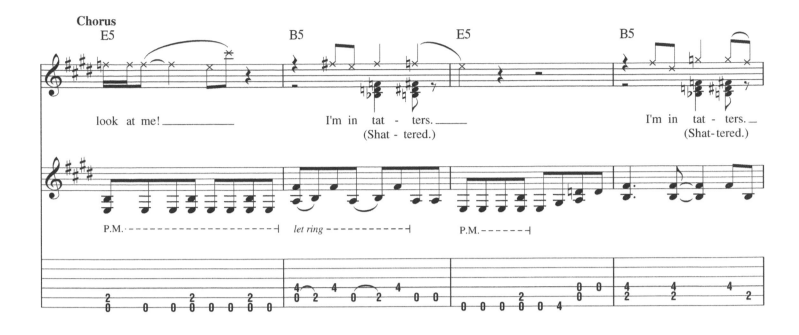

Chorus

look at me! _____   I'm in tat - ters. _____   I'm in tat - ters. _
(Shat - tered.)   (Shat-tered.)

P.M. ------------------------| *let ring* ----------| P.M. ------|

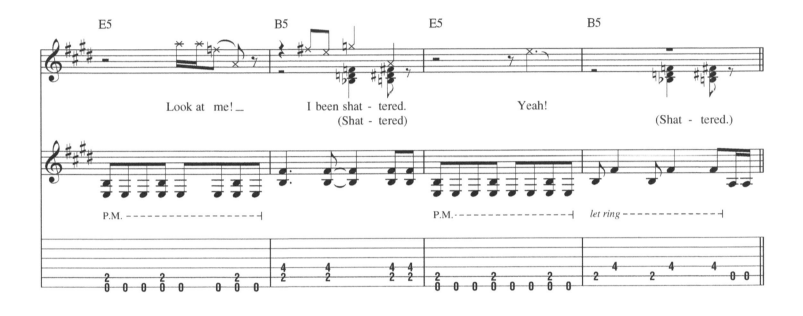

Look at me! _   I been shat - tered.   Yeah!   (Shat - tered.)
(Shat - tered)

P.M. ----------------------| P.M. ----------------| *let ring* -------------|

Verse

3. *Spoken:* Pride and joy and greed and sex,   that's what makes our town the best. __   Pride and joy and dirt - y dreams are

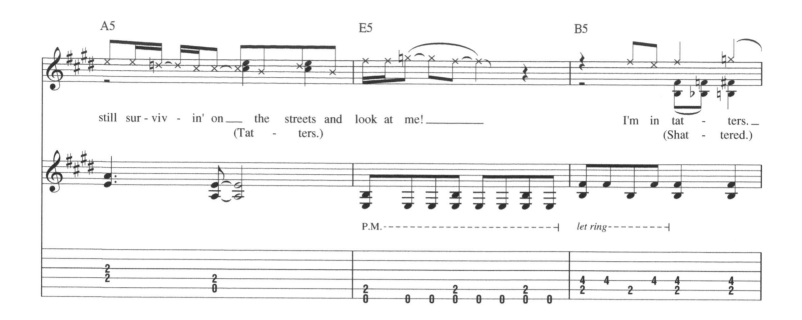

Does it mat - ter? ___   Uh huh.   I'm, uh, shat - tered. ___

Pile it up!   Pile it high ___ on the plat - ter!
(Sha - doo - bee.)   (Shat - tered.)   (Shat tered.)

Additional Lyrics

Outro   Mm. I'm shattered. Huh! Sha-doo-bee. Shattered.
Huh! Sha-doo-bee. Shattered.
Sha-doo-bee. (Shattered. Shattered.)
Don't you know the crime rate's goin' up, up, up, up, up?
To live in this town you must be tough, tough, tough, tough, tough, tough, tough.
(Shattered. Shattered.) We got rats on the West Side, bedbugs uptown.
What a mess! This town's in tatters.
I been shattered. My brain's been battered,
Splattered all over Manhattan. Uh, huh.
What say? Sha-doo-bee. Uh, huh.
This town's full of money grabbers.
Go ahead! Bite the Big Apple. Don't mind the maggots!
Uh, huh. (Shattered.) Sha-doo-bee. My brain's been battered!
My fam'ly come around 'n' flatter, flatter, flatter, flatter, flatter, flatter, flatter.
Pile it up! (Shattered.) Pile it up. (Sha-doo-bee.)
Pile it high on the platter!

Refugee

Words and Music by Tom Petty and Mike Campbell

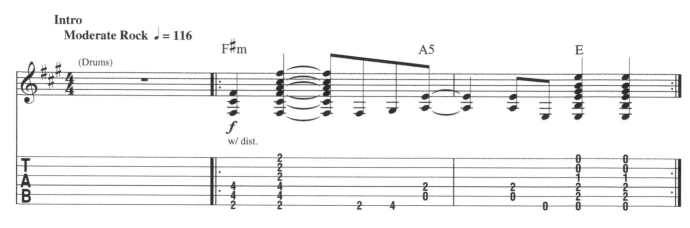

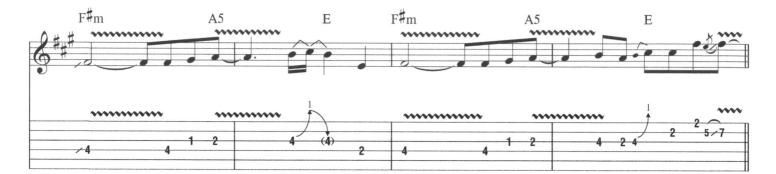

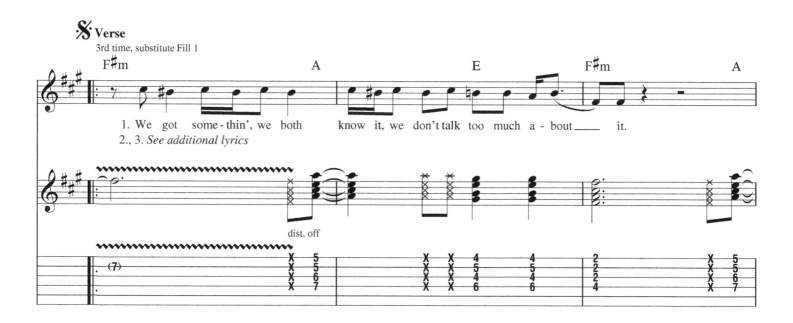

1. We got some-thin', we both know it, we don't talk too much a - bout_____ it.
2., 3. *See additional lyrics*

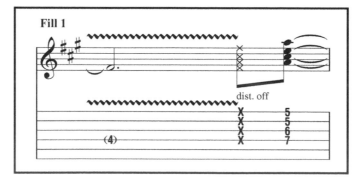

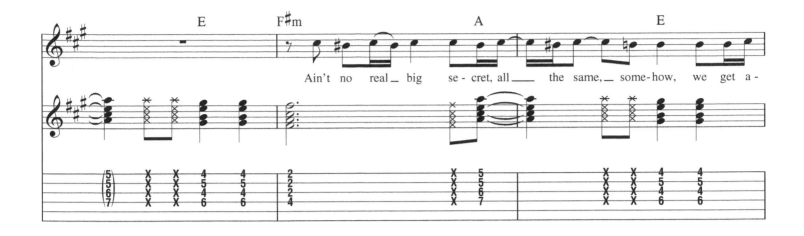

Ain't no real big se - cret, all the same, some - how, we get a -

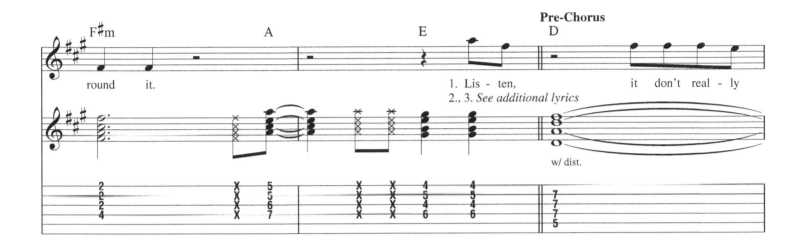

round it. 1. Lis - ten, it don't real - ly
2., 3. *See additional lyrics*
w/ dist.

Pre-Chorus

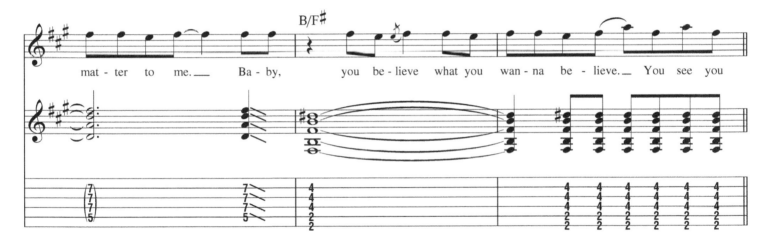

mat - ter to me. Ba - by, you be - lieve what you wan - na be - lieve. You see you

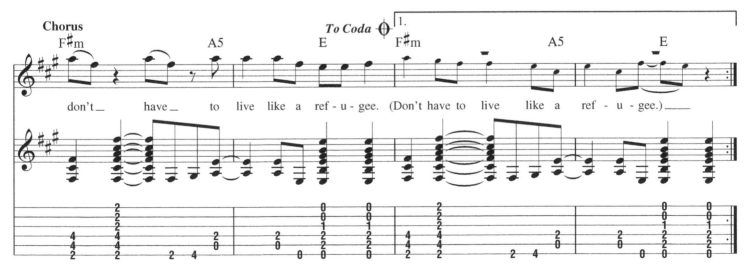

Chorus

To Coda

1.

don't have to live like a ref - u - gee. (Don't have to live like a ref - u - gee.)

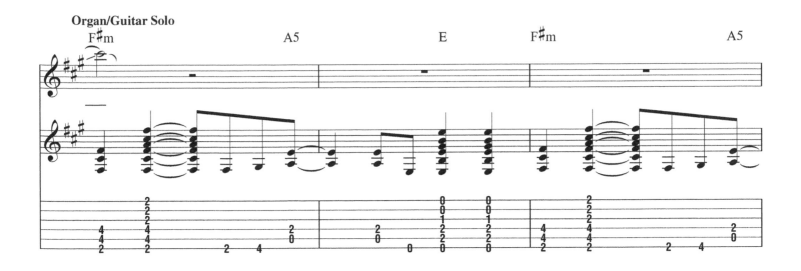

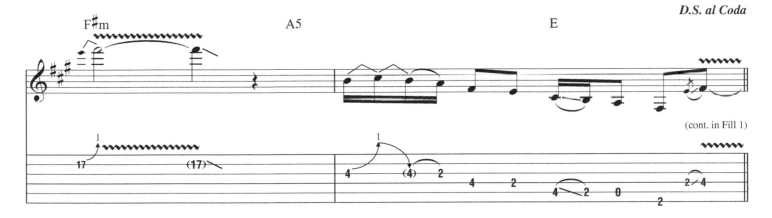

D.S. al Coda

(cont. in Fill 1)

(Don't have to live like a ref - u - gee.)___ No, you don't have ___ to

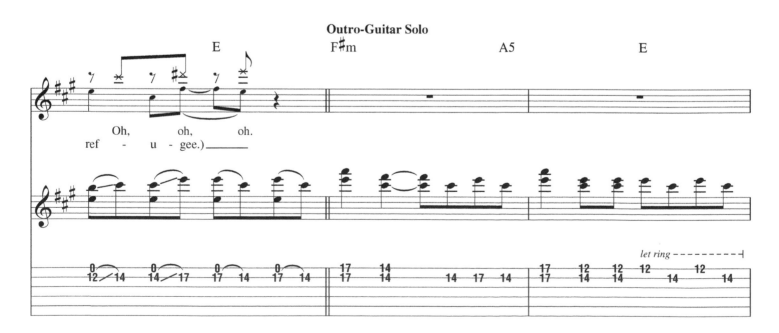

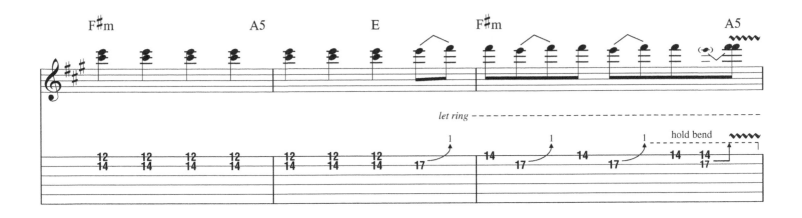

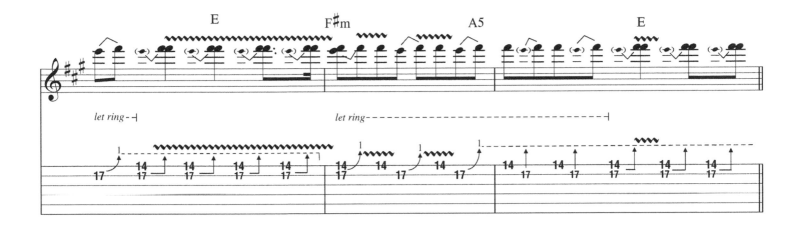

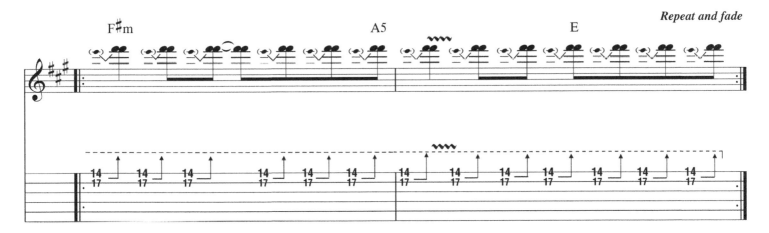

Additional Lyrics

2. Somewhere, somehow, somebody must have
   Kicked you around some.
   Tell me why you wanna lay there,
   Revel in your abandon.

Pre-Chorus 2. Honey, it don't make no diff'rence to me.
   Baby, ev'rybody's had to fight to be free.

3. Somewhere, somehow, somebody must have
   Kicked you around some.
   Who knows? Maybe you were kidnapped,
   Tied up, taken away and held for ransom.

Pre-Chorus 3. Honey, it don't really matter to me.
   Baby, ev'rybody's had to fight to be free.

Sunshine of Your Love

Words and Music by Jack Bruce, Pete Brown and Eric Clapton

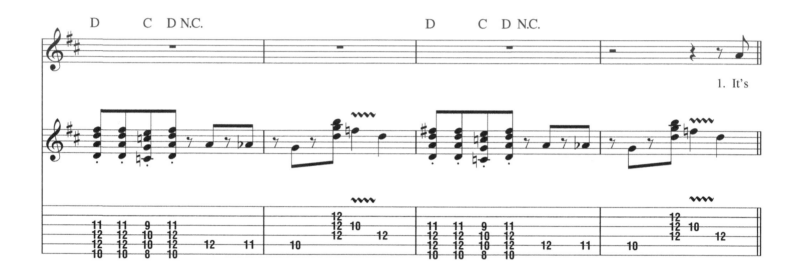

soon be with you, _ my _ love, _ to give you my dawn _ sur - prise. _____ I'll

be with you, dar - ling, soon. _____ I'll be with you when _ the stars _ start _ fall - ing.

To Coda ⊕

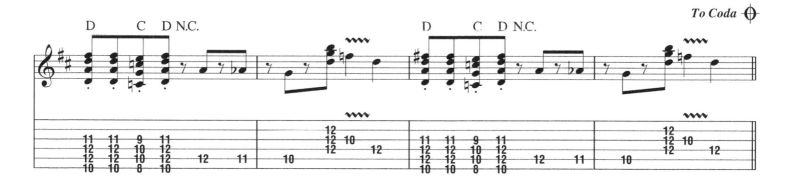

Chorus

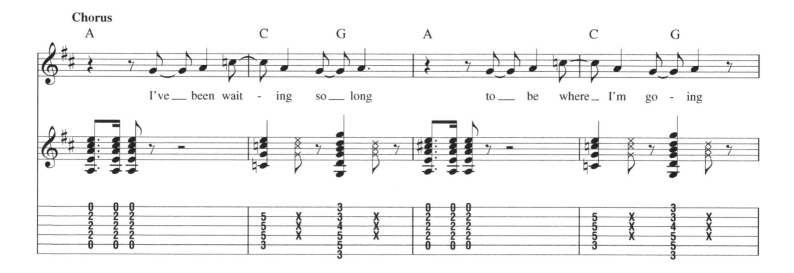

I've _ been wait - ing so _ long to _ be where _ I'm go - ing

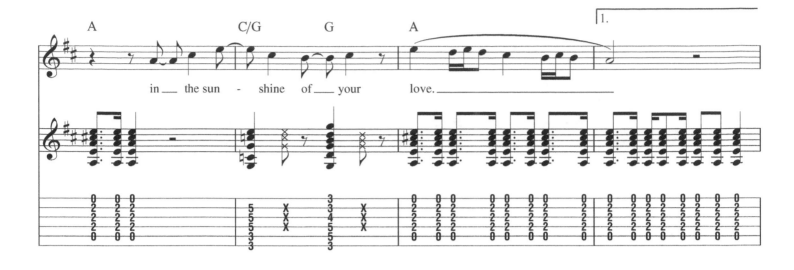

in ___ the sun - shine of ___ your love. _____

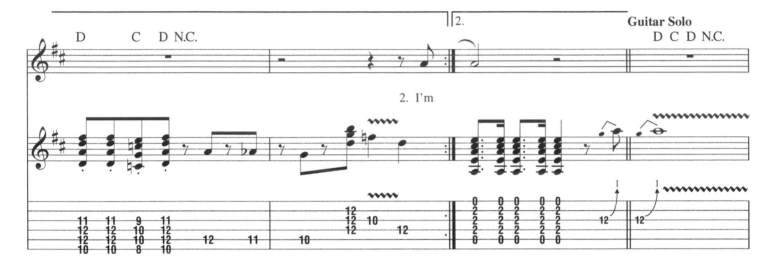

2. I'm

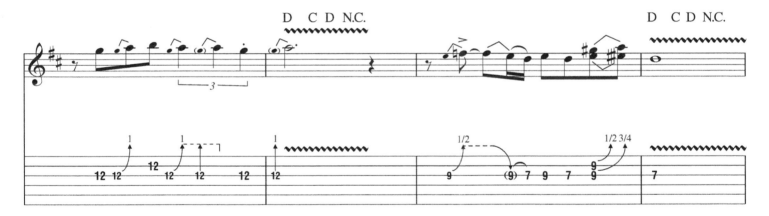

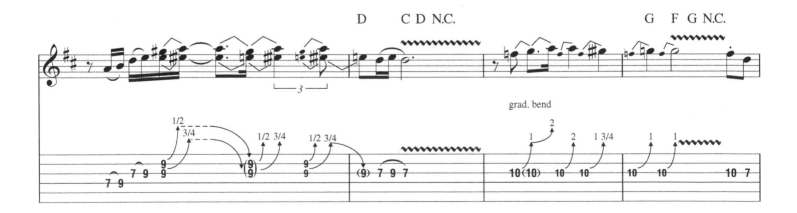

grad. bend

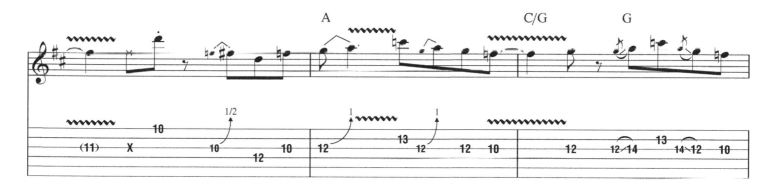

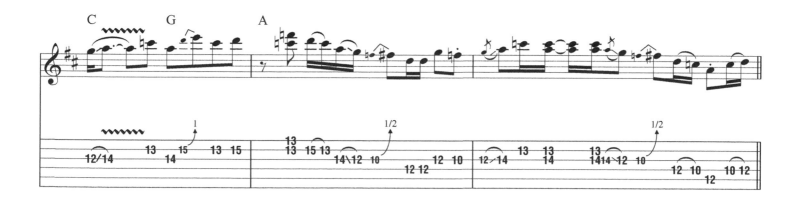

Additional Lyrics

2., 3. I'm with you, my love;
The light shining through on you.
Yes, I'm with you, my love.
It's the morning and just we two.
I'll stay with you, darling, now.
I'll stay with you till my seeds are dried up.

Tush

Words and Music by Billy F Gibbons, Dusty Hill and Frank Beard

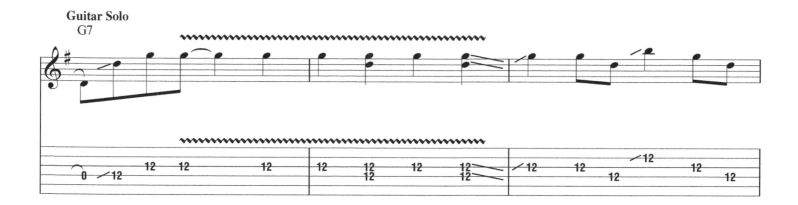

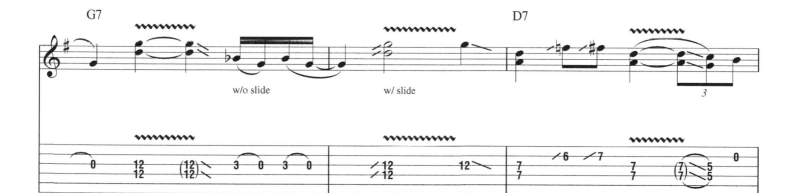

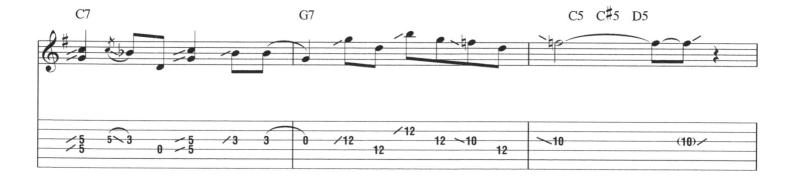

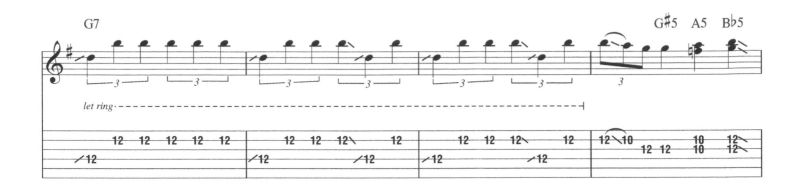

3. Take me back,

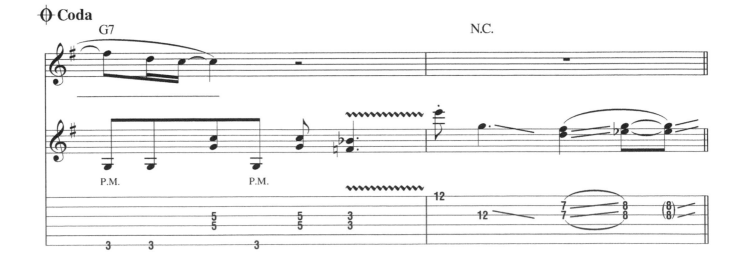

Outro-Guitar Solo

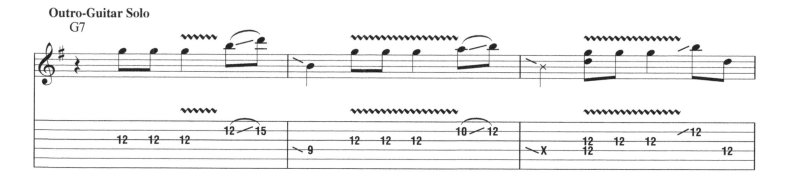

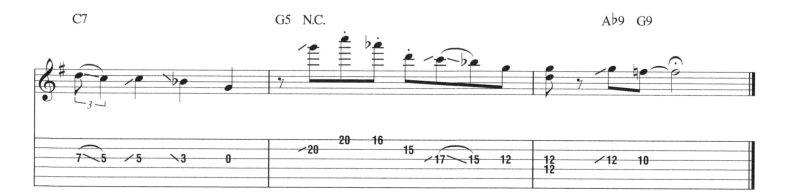

Additional Lyrics

2. I've been bad, I've been good,
   Dallas, Texas, Hollywood.
   I ain't askin' for much. Mm.
   I said, Lord, take me downtown.
   I'm just lookin' for some tush.

3. Take me back, way back home,
   Not by myself, not alone.
   I ain't askin' for much. Mm.
   I said, Lord, take me downtown.
   I'm just lookin' for some tush.

Takin' Care of Business

Words and Music by Randy Bachman

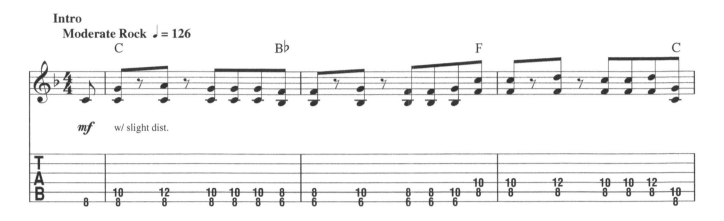

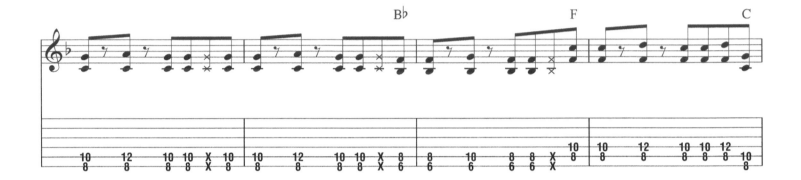

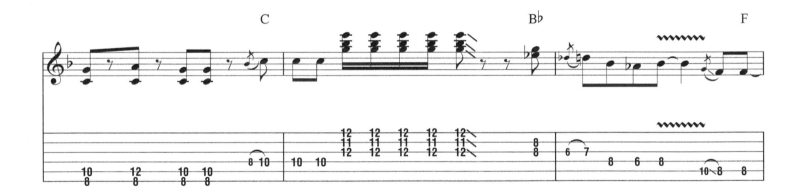

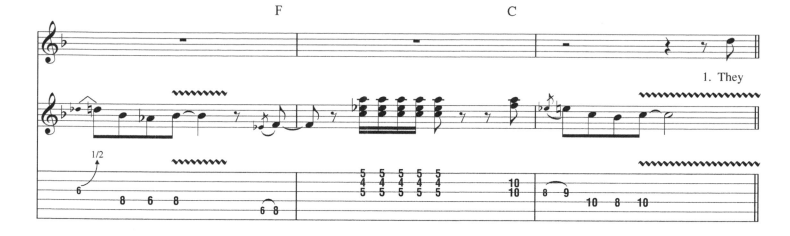

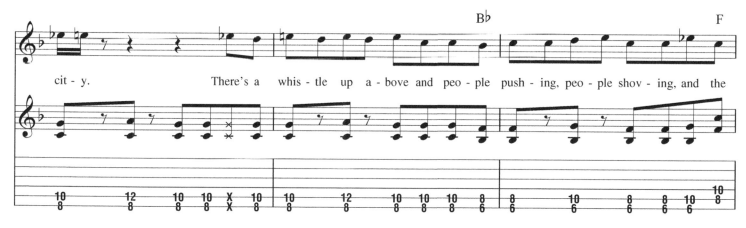

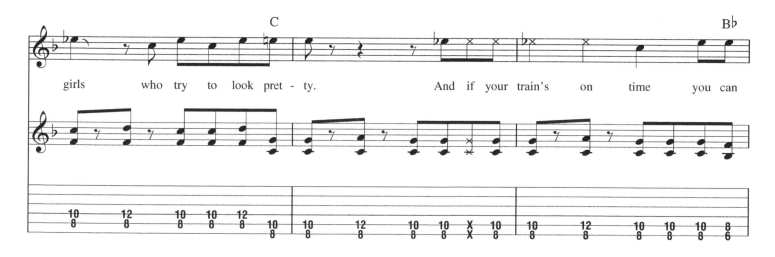

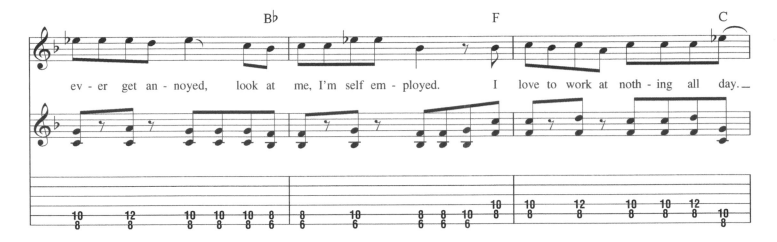

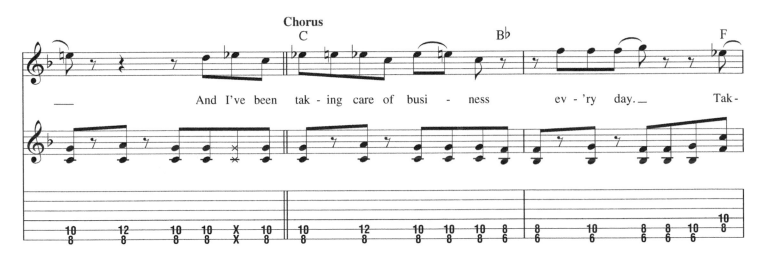

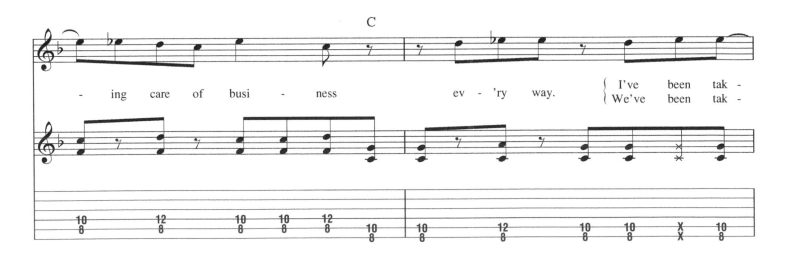

- ing care of busi - ness, }
- ing care of busi - ness, } it's all mine.___ Tak - ing care of busi - ness and

To Coda ⊕ | 1.
Interlude

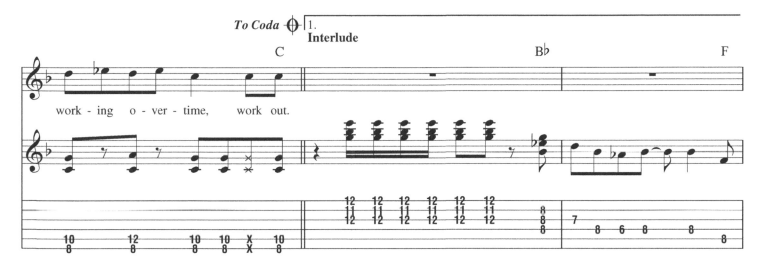

work - ing o - ver - time, work out.

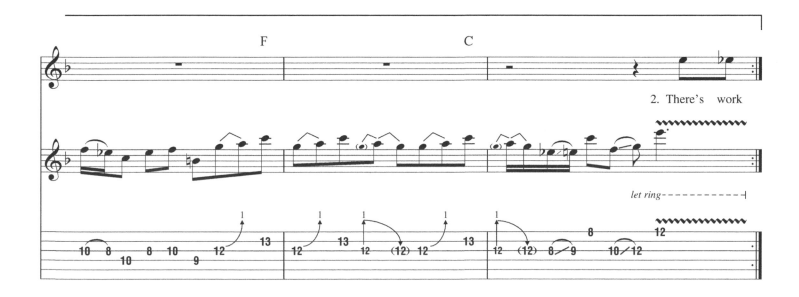

2. There's work

let ring- - - - - - - - - - -|

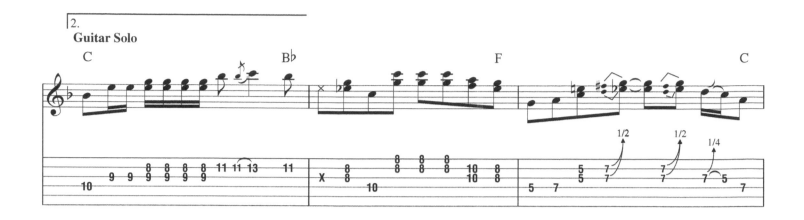

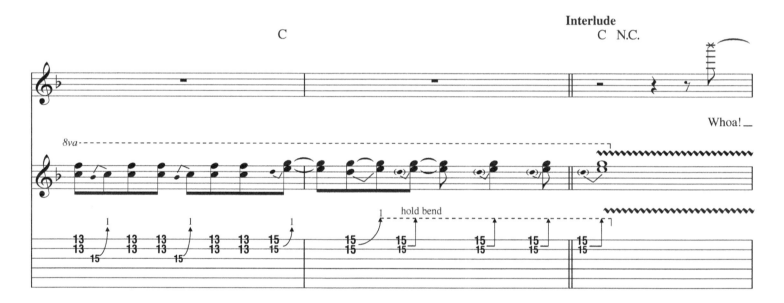

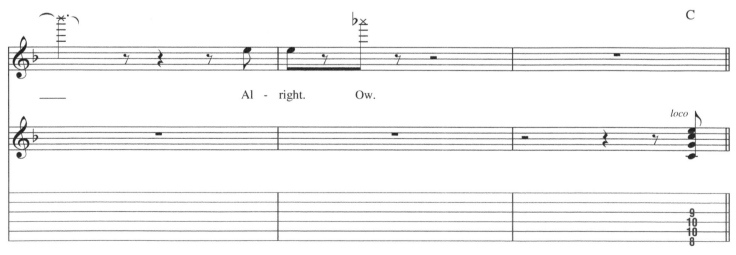

Bridge

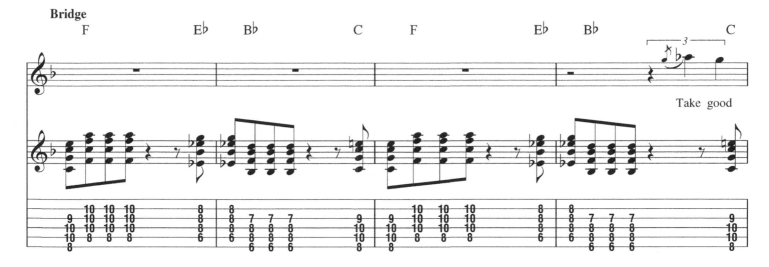

Take good

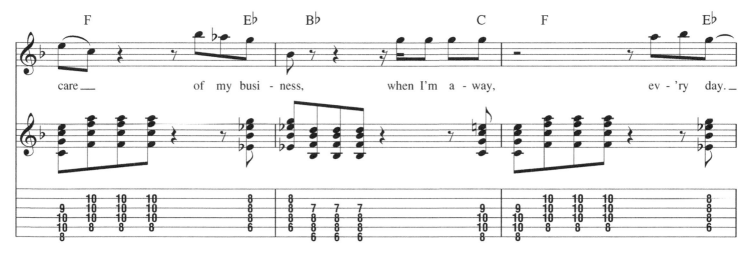

care ___ of my busi - ness, when I'm a - way, ev - 'ry day. ___

Guitar Solo

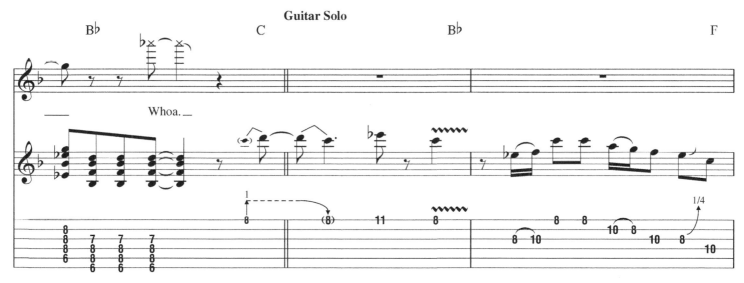

Whoa. ___

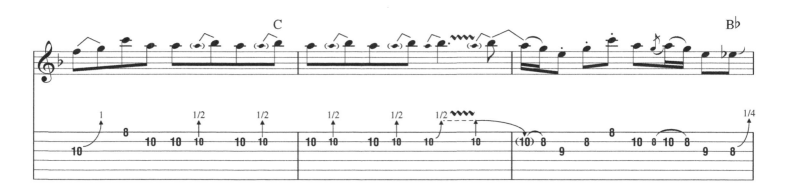

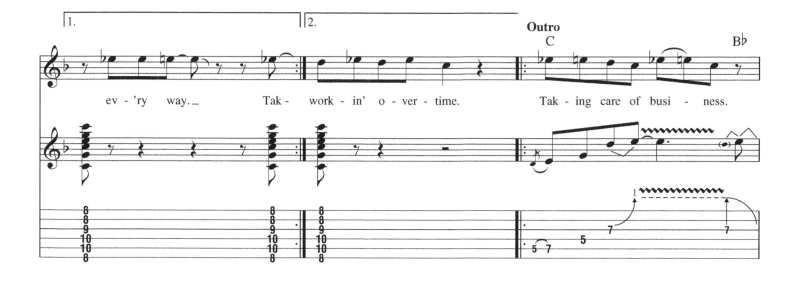

ev - 'ry way.___ Tak - work - in' o - ver - time.

Outro

Tak - ing care of busi - ness.

Tak - ing care of busi - ness.

We've been tak -

Repeat and fade

- ing care of busi - ness.

We've been tak - ing care of busi - ness.

Tak-

Additional Lyrics

2. There's work easy as fishin', you could be a musician,
   If you could make sounds loud or mellow.
   Get a second hand guitar, chances are you'll go far
   If you get in with the right group of fellows.
   People see you having fun just a lying in the sun.
   Tell them that you like it this way.
   It's the work that we avoid and we're all self employed.
   We love to work at nothing all day.
   And we've been...

Walk This Way

Words and Music by Steven Tyler and Joe Perry

cheer - lead - er, was a real young bleed - er all the times I could rem - i - nisce,___ 'cause the

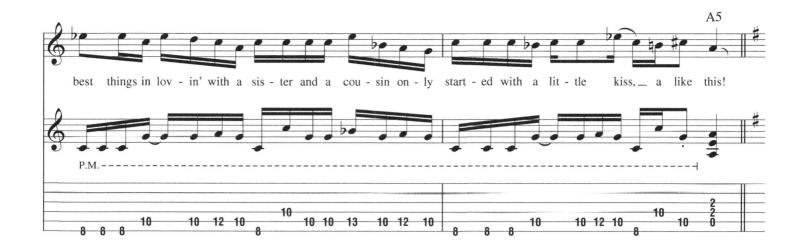

best things in lov - in' with a sis - ter and a cou - sin on - ly start - ed with a lit - tle kiss,___ a like this!

A5

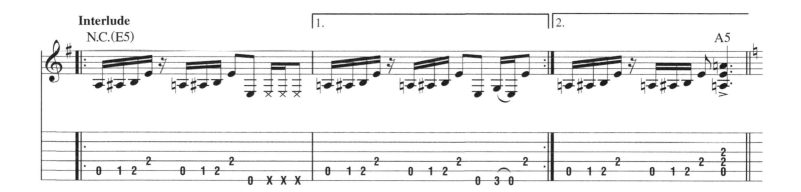

Interlude

N.C.(E5)

1.

2.

A5

Verse

N.C.(C7)

2., 4. See - saw swing - in' with the boys in the school and your feet fly - in' up in the air,___ I sing,

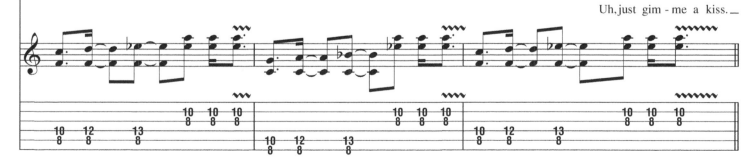

Guitar Solo

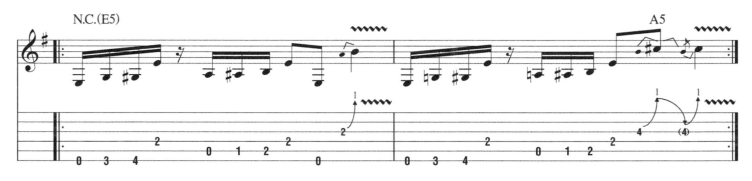

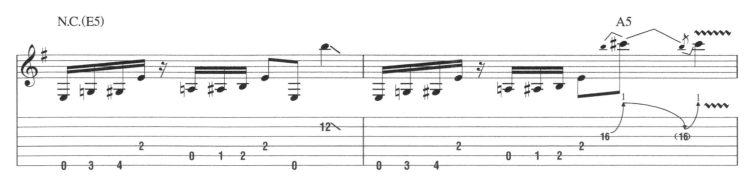

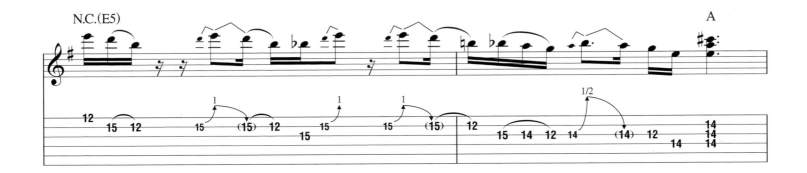

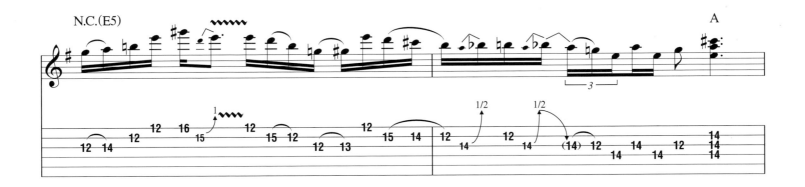

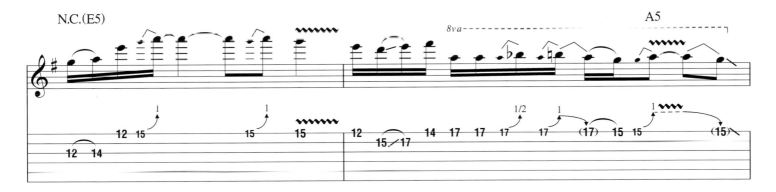

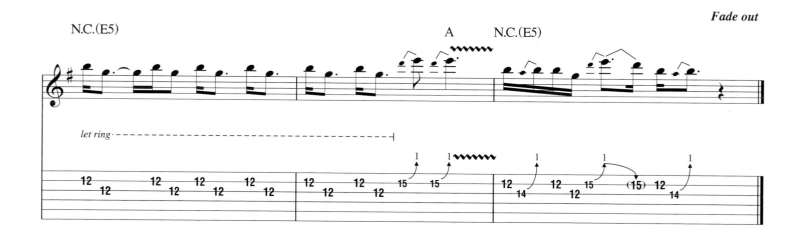

Additional Lyrics

3. School girl skinny with a classy kind a sassy little skirt's climbin' way up her knee,
   There was three young ladies in the school gym locker when I noticed they was lookin' at me.
   I was in high school loser, never made it with a lady till the boys told me somethin' I missed,
   Then my next door neighbor with a daughter had a favor so I gave her just a little kiss, a like this!